Schwarzwald

Holger Spiering **Schwarzwald**

EDITION**PANORAMA**BIBLIOTHEK

Meinen Eltern, für die dort alles begann …

Schwarzwald

Iris Lemanczyk

Dunkler Tann. Im Gegenlicht erscheinen Berge und Bäume finster, geradezu schwarz. Schwarzer Wald. Rau ist das größte deutsche Mittelgebirge, das sich über 160 Kilometer von Pforzheim bis Basel erstreckt. Rau, aber auch lieblich und verträumt. Urig und urtümlich. Mit steilwandigen Schluchten, durch die wilde Bäche rauschen und in sanften Talmulden tiefblaue Karseen ruhen. Bizarre Felsgruppen, spektakuläre Wasserfälle, kahle Berggipfel, erdige Moore. Der Duft von Harz. Langsam steigen die Nebel zur Sonne empor, dann ist die Stunde der Waldgeister um. Das Spiel des Lichts macht die Landschaft immer verträumter: sanftgrüne Hügel, saftige Bergwiesen, romantische Bachtäler.

„Die Wälder sind so dicht und still, so tannig und duftend. (...) Ein sattes, dauerhaftes Dämmerlicht fällt in die säulenbestandenen Gänge, so dass die verirrten Sonnensprenkel, die hier auf einen Stamm und dort auf einen Ast treffen, kräftig hervortreten und das Moos regelrecht zu brennen scheint. Aber die eigentümlichste und zauberhafteste Wirkung bringt das weich gestreute Licht der tief stehenden Nachmittagssonne hervor. Kein einziger Strahl kann dann eindringen, das weiche Licht aber erfüllt alles mit einem zarten grünen Dunst, der Theaterbeleuchtung des Märchenlandes", schrieb der amerikanische Schriftsteller Mark Twain 1880 über den Schwarzwald.

Doch die Namen zwischen den schattigen Tannen- und Fichtenwäldern klingen alles andere als lieblich und verträumt: „Höllental", „Nothschrei", „Zuflucht", „Siehdichfür", „Bärental", „Wutach" oder „Wolfach" deuten nicht gerade auf eine liebliche Gegend hin. Lange war der schwarze Wald Wildnis. Urwald. Ein undurchdringliches Meer aus Holz.

Die Römer sahen ihn als unliebsames, unzugängliches, ja unheimliches Hindernis, in dem Elche, Bären und Auerochsen den Ton angaben. Nur die Thermalquellen am Westrand des Schwarzwaldes wussten sie zu schätzen. Dort schlugen sie nicht nur ihre Zelte auf, sondern gründeten gleich Städte an den warmen Quellbädern: Ettlingen, Baden-Baden und Badenweiler gehören dazu.

Zu den frühen Siedlern, die sich in diese finstere, unheimliche Wildnis vorwagten, gehören mutige Mönche. Das Kloster St. Trudbert im Münstertal ist eine der frühesten Siedlungen und wird im 7. Jahrhundert erwähnt. Klostergründungen in Hirsau, Alpirsbach und Enzklösterle folgten. Nach den Klöstern versuchte auch der Adel, sich Teile des Schwarzwaldes einzuverleiben. Die Zähringer etablierten sich im tannenübersäten „Nigra Silva". Von den Rändern her begann man zu roden und nahm sich an Holz, was man brauchte. Zum Bauen oder Heizen, ansonsten galt der Wald als denkbar überflüssig. Mit dem 14. Jahrhundert setzte jedoch eine gezielte Nutzung der Wälder ein. Erste Sägemühlen entstanden genauso wie Glashütten.

Später etablierte sich der Holzhandel im großen Stil. „Sie handeln mit ihrem Wald. Sie fällen und behauen die Tannen, flößen sie durch die Nagold in den Neckar und von dem oberen Neckar den Rhein hinab, bis weit hinein nach Holland, und am Meer kennt man die Schwarzwälder und ihre langen Flöße. Sie halten an jeder Stadt, die am Strom liegt und erwarten stolz, ob man Balken und Bretter abkaufen werde. Ihre stärksten und längsten Balken aber verhandeln sie um schweres Geld an die Mynheers, welche Schiffe daraus bauen", schrieb Wilhelm Hauff in seiner Erzählung „Das kalte Herz".

Nur auf den Wasserwegen konnten die riesigen Baumstämme aus dem Gebirgswald zu den Handelsplätzen an Neckar und Rhein geschafft werden. Zunächst schleppten Pferde die geschlagenen Stämme ans Ufer eines flößbaren Wasserlaufs. Manchmal warf man das Holz einfach ins Wasser, kleinere Stämme fanden so allein den Weg zu den Auffangplätzen. Aber die Flößer banden auch mächtige Stämme zusammen. Dann sprangen sie auf die aneinander gebundenen Baumstämme, flößten darauf über Staustufen, an Flussbiegungen vorbei und über den felsigen Untergrund. Ein lebensgefährlicher Beruf, der enorm viel Kraft und Geschick erforderte. Nicht umsonst erhielten die Flößer von den Waldbesitzern einen überdurchschnittlichen Lohn. Meist war Holland, mit seinem immensen Holzbedarf für den Schiffsbau, das Ziel. Deshalb hießen die mächtigen Baumstämme mit bis zu zwanzig Meter Länge „Holländer".

Ein anderer Schwarzwald-Beruf, der mit Reisen verbunden war, war der Uhrenträger. Die Schwarzwalduhr war schon im 18. Jahrhundert ein Exportschlager und wanderte auf den Rücken der Uhrenträger bis nach Paris, Istanbul und St. Petersburg. Franz Ketterer aus Schönwald erfand um 1740 die erste Schwarzwälder Kuckucksuhr im fürchterlich langen Winter, in dem es kaum Arbeit gab. Hartnäckig hält sich die Geschichte vom Uhrmachermeister, der einen jungen, aus dem Nest gefallenen Kuckuck mit nach Hause nahm und pflegte. In der Werkstatt schrie der Vogel immer zur vollen Stunde „Kuckuck". Schließlich schnitzte der Uhrmacher ihm eine eigene Uhr. Andere behaupten, die Kuckucke galten als Glücksbringer, darum landeten sie in der Uhr. Wie auch immer, so brachte sich damit eine Region, die nichts besaß außer Holz und gesunder Luft, in Lohn und Brot.

Später, im Zeitalter der Eisenbahn, ging die Fracht auf den Gleisen zu Häfen und per Schiff in alle Welt. 1893 war die „cuckoo clock" Star der Industrieausstellung in Chicago. Amerikaner entdeckten den „black forest".

Der junge Ernest Hemingway kam zum Forellenfischen nach Triberg. Mark Twain hielt sich zum Wandern und Beobachten von Land und Leuten im Schwarzwald auf. Völlig fasziniert berichtet er: „Wenn man einmal anfängt, an einer solchen Stelle hinunterzurollen, gibt es kein Halten, bis man den Grund erreicht. Man stelle sich bloß vor, dass Leute auf einer Schräge Landwirtschaft betreiben, die so steil ist, dass man im günstigsten Fall davon sagen kann, sie ist ein bisschen steiler als eine Stehleiter und nicht ganz so steil wie ein Mansardendach. Aber sie tun es wirklich."

Die steilen Hänge hatten und haben einen großen Vorzug. Sie sind ideal fürs Ski- und Schlittenfahren, zumindest fürs Hinabgleiten. 1891 schickte Nordpolforscher Fridtjof Nansen Skier aus Norwegen in den Schwarzwald. Postboten waren die Ersten, die sie bekamen, um die weit abgelegenen Höfe auch im Winter erreichen zu können. Im selben Jahr gründen Skibegeisterte den ersten Skiverein überhaupt, den Ski-Club Todtnau.

Passend dazu entwickelte der Bauer, Gastwirt und Tüftler Robert Winterhalder aus Schollach eine Seiltriebtechnik der Mühlen weiter und ließ sich die „Vorrichtung zum Hinaufziehen von Schneeschuhläufern und Rodlern mittels einer kontinuierlich sich bewegenden Seilbahn auf beschneiten Berghängen" patentieren – der erste Skilift der Welt. Er stand nicht in Davos oder Garmisch, sondern neben Winterhalders „Schneckenhof" und konnte Rodler und Skifahrer 280 Meter den Berg hochziehen.

Der Wintertourismus im Schwarzwald erreichte damit eine neue Dimension. Heute tummeln sich allein auf dem Feldberg, dem mit 1493 Metern höchsten Gipfel des Schwarzwaldes, im Winter Tausende von Skifahrern, Snowboardern und Langläufern. Hier herrscht Massenbetrieb, vom unwiderstehlichen Charme tiefverschneiter Höhenzüge, von Einsamkeit und Ruhe weit entfernt.

Auch im Sommer, wenn der Schwarzwald ein Wanderparadies ist, muss man heutzutage oft tief in den Wald hineinwandern, um Ruhe und Einsamkeit zu finden. Der Tourismus, der aus einer romantischen Naturbegeisterung entstanden ist, hat nach und nach alle Gebiete erobert, die früher unwegsam und einsam waren.

Und dennoch bleibt eine Wanderung durch die Wutachschlucht, den „Grand Canyon" des schwarzen Waldes ein einmaliges Erlebnis. Die Wutach, wild, urig, der letzte ungezähmte Wildfluss der deutschen Mittelgebirge. Eine Insel ursprünglicher Natur, in der das Wasser eine tiefe Schlucht durch den Muschelkalk gegraben hat. Vor allem im Frühjahr, während der Schneeschmelze macht die Wutach ihrem Namen alle Ehre. Manchmal verlegt sie kurzerhand ihren Lauf. Berge von Holz und Geröll türmen sich an ihren Ufern auf. Felswände werden unterspült, sodass neue Kiesbänke entstehen. Im Sommer gibt sich die Wutach eher zahm. 24 Kilometer Wanderweg sind es dann von Lenzkirch-Kappel bis zur Wutachmühle. Um die Wutach nicht aus ihrem ökologischen Gleichgewicht zu bringen, ist der Zugang kontingentiert. Ein überwältigendes Naturerlebnis ist die Schlucht: An die 500 Schmetterlingsarten gaukeln über 1200 Pflanzenarten, darunter viele Orchideen. Mehr als hundert Vogelarten sind hier heimisch, darunter der Turmfalke und der Eisvogel.

Nicht nur Natur pur herrscht im Schwarzwald, es gibt eine Vielzahl von Städten. Bad Wildbad, zum Beispiel. Hier suchten Menschen bereits vor 600 Jahren Heilung. Sein Wasser hilft gegen Erschöpfung und eine aus dem Tritt geratene Gesundheit, heißt es. Selbst die rheumatisch steifen Reitpferde von Blaublütigen sollen hier gekurt haben.

Oder Freudenstadt, die höchstgelegene Stadt im Schwarzwald mit dem größten Marktplatz Deutschlands. Herzog Friedrich I. von Württemberg ließ ihn 1599 anlegen – und um ihn die Stadt herum. Eigentlich plante er in der Mitte des Platzes seine Residenz, doch sie wurde nie gebaut. Protestantische Glaubensflüchtlinge sollten der herzoglichen Verheißung auf ein besseres Leben folgen und der Region zum Aufschwung verhelfen.

Die mondäne Schöne ist Baden-Baden, lange Zeit Sommerresidenz von Geld- und Hochadel. Prinzen waren hier auf Brautschau. Grafen brachten sich im Kasino um Vermögen und Ehre. Generäle erholten sich im irisch-römischen Kuppelbau des Friedrichsbades. Mark Twain durchschaute das muntere Kurgasttreiben „voll von Schein und Aufgeblasenheit".

Ganz ohne Aufgeblasenheit kommt dagegen die schwäbisch-alemannische Fasnet oder Fasnacht aus. Im Schwarzwald ist die Fasnet bäuerlich. Mehr bunt als glanzvoll. Bodenständig und derb, voll von uralten Ritualen. Vom „schmotzigen Dunschtig" bis Aschermittwoch verwandeln sich Männer und Frauen in zottelige Fabeltiere, springlebendige Hansele und Hexen mit schrecklichen Masken, die hier Larven heißen. Die Luft ist erfüllt vom Lärm der Rätschen, vom Scheppern der Nussschalen an den Gewändern und dem Klang der Schellen. In Schramberg versuchen tollkühne Männer in wackligen Waschzubern die Schiltach hinabzuschippern. In Rottweil springen die Narren durchs Schwarze Tor. In Elzach toben die feuerroten „Schuttig" durch die Gassen. Jeder Ort hat seine Geschichten, Rituale und „Kleidle", die über Generationen weitervererbt werden.

Trotz alter Traditionen, Trubel und Tourismus landet man immer wieder auf einer einsamen Waldlichtung, bei stillen Seen, in malerischen Winkeln und in gesunder Luft. Ein Drittel aller heilklimatischen Kurorte befinden sich im Reizklima des Schwarzwaldes, bei dem in den Höhen ausgeprägte Temperaturunterschiede, lange Sonnenscheindauer und reine Luft für den Reiz des Klimas sorgen.

Egal ob wandern im dunklen Tann, durch enge Schluchten, Moore oder sonnendurchflutete Wiesen, egal ob den Fernblick über Berg und Tal auf der Schwarzwald Hochstraße oder auf dem Westweg schweifen lassend, ob durch verschneite Loipen eine Langlaufspur ziehend, in warmen Thermalquellen aalend, oder die Schwarzwälder Kirschtorte, jene mächtige Anhäufung aus Sahne, Kirschen und schnapsgetränktem Biskuit, genießend. Egal ob am Mummel- oder Titisee, im Kinzigtal oder auf der Hornisgrinde, urig und urtümlich, wild und romantisch ist der Schwarzwald noch immer. Seinem Charme und Zauber kann man sich nicht entziehen.

Black Forest

Iris Lemanczyk

Sombre pine forest. Against the light, the mountains and trees glower darkly, even black. The Black Forest. Germany's longest mountain range, which extends over 100 miles from Pforzheim to Basel, is rough and bleak. Rough, but also mellow and dreamlike. Untouched and primeval. With steep-walled ravines, through which babbling brooks rush, and where deep-blue mountain cirques collect in shallow coombs. Bizarre rock formations, spectacular waterfalls, barren mountain peaks, earthy moorland. The scent of tree sap and resin. Slowly the mists rise up into the sunlight, and the hour of the forest spirits is now over. The play of the light makes the landscape ever more dreamlike: soft green hills, lush mountain meadows, romantic stream valleys.

"The forests are so dense and silent, everywhere the scent of pine. (...) A deep, permanent twilight lies between the tree-lined paths, so that errant beams of sunlight, falling here on a trunk and there on a bough, stand out vividly, and the moss appears as if on fire. But the strangest and most magical effect is caused by the soft and diffuse light of the late afternoon sun. No single ray of light can then penetrate the canopy, but the pale light suffuses and envelops everything with a delicate green aura, the theatre lighting of fairyland", wrote the American author Mark Twain in 1880 about the Black Forest.

Yet the names between the shadowy pine and spruce forests sound anything but charming and dreamlike: "Höllental" (hell valley), "Nothschrei" (outcry), "Zuflucht" (refuge), "Siehdichfür" (look-out), "Bärental" (bear valley), "Wutach" (~ raging stream) or "Wolfach" (~ wolf stream) hardly indicate an area noted for its charm. The Black Forest remained a wilderness for a long time. Primeval forest. An impenetrable sea of wood.

The Romans regarded it as an unwelcoming, inaccessible, even sinister obstacle, inhabited by elk, bears and aurochs. The only thing they found to like about it were the thermal springs along the western edge of the forest. Here they not only pitched camp, but quickly established settlements and towns around these warm springs, such as Ettlingen, Baden-Baden and Badenweiler.

Amongst the early settlers who ventured into these dark and forbidding wilds were courageous monks. The cloister of St. Trudbert in the Münster valley was one of the first settlements, and was first mentioned in records in the 7th Century. This was followed by the foundation of cloisters in Hirsau, Alpirsbach and Enzklösterle. After the monks, the nobility also tried to take control of parts of the Black Forest. The Zähringers established themselves in the pine-strewn "Nigra Silva". Starting from the edges, people began to clear the forest, taking whatever they needed in the way of wood for building or heating, otherwise the forest was considered good for nothing. In the 14th Century however, the forest began to be exploited commercially. The first sawmills were built, together with glassworks.

The timber trade later developed on an even larger scale. "They trade in their forest. They fell and hew the pines, float them down the Nagold into the Neckar and from the upper Neckar down the Rhine, downriver as far as Holland, and at the sea one can tell those from the Black Forest from their long rafts of logs. They stop at every town along the river, and wait proudly for people to come and buy beams and planks from them. The strongest and longest beams however are sold for large sums to the Mynheers (the Dutch), who build ships with them", wrote Wilhelm Hauff in his novella "Das kalte Herz" ("The Cold Heart").

The huge tree trunks from the upland forests could only be transported to the trading centres on the Neckar and Rhine by water. First the felled trunks were dragged by horses to the banks of the nearest floatable water course. Sometimes the wood was simply thrown into the water, so that smaller trunks found their own way to the collection points. But the log-drivers also bound together large tree trunks. They then jumped onto the rafts, floating downriver on them over weirs, around bends in the river and over the rocky riverbed. A perilous profession, which demanded enormous strength and great skill. Not for nothing did the log-drivers receive from the owners of the forest an above-average wage. Holland, with its huge demand for timber for shipbuilding, was usually the destination. The huge tree trunks up to 60 ft. in length and more, were therefore called "Holländer".

Another Black Forest profession which involved travelling was the clock-carrier. The Black Forest clock was already an export hit by the 18th Century, and travelled on the back of the clock-carrier as far as Paris, Istanbul and St. Petersburg. Franz Ketterer from Schönwald invented the first Black Forest cuckoo-clock around 1740, in the terribly long winter when there was little other work to do. The story persists of the master clockmaker who found a young cuckoo which had fallen out of the nest, took it home and cared for it. In the workshop, the bird cried out "cuckoo" every hour on the hour. Finally, the clockmaker carved the bird its own clock. Others claim that cuckoos were considered as omens of good fortune, and therefore ended up in the clock. Whatever the truth, this earned money and food for a region which had no other resources except for wood and healthy air.

Later, during the era of the railway, the freight went by rail to the ports, and then by ship all over the world. In 1893, the "cuckoo clock" became the star of the industrial exhibition in Chicago. Americans discovered the "Black Forest".

The young Ernest Hemingway came to Triberg for the trout fishing. Mark Twain stayed in the Black Forest to trek around and observe the country and its people. Completely fascinated, he reported: "If one ever starts to roll downhill at such a place, there is no stopping until you reach the bottom. Just imagine people trying to carry out agriculture on a slope which is so steep that the best one could say of it is that it is a bit steeper than a step-ladder, and not quite so steep as a mansard roof. But in fact they do it."

The steep slopes had, and still have one great advantage. They are ideal for skiing and sledging, at least downhill. In 1891, the North Pole explorer Fridtjof Nansen sent skis from Norway to the Black Forest. Postmen were the first to be issued with them in order to be able to reach the remote farms in the winter. In the same year, enthusiastic skiers founded the first ever ski club, the Todtnau Ski Club.

Around the same time, the farmer, innkeeper and part-time inventor Robert Winterhalder from Schollach, further developed a cable drive mechanism used in mills, and had it patented as a "device for pulling skiers and sledgers up snow-covered mountain slopes by means of a continually moving cableway" – the world's first ski lift. It was not in Davos or Garmisch, but next to Winterhalder's farm, the "Schneckenhof", and could pull sledgers and skiers over 900 ft. up the mountain.

This brought a new dimension to winter tourism in the Black Forest. Today, the Feldberg alone, at nearly 5,000 ft. the highest peak in the Black Forest, attracts thousands of skiers, snowboarders and cross-country skiers to the Black Forest every winter. This is now a mass tourist business, far removed from the irresistible charm of snow-covered mountains, solitude and calm.

In the summer too, when the Black Forest becomes a paradise for trekkers and ramblers, one often has to make one's way deep into the woods

these days in order to find calm and solitude. The tourism which developed from a romantic love of nature has gradually conquered all those areas which were previously inaccessible and remote.
Yet a hike through the Wutach Gorge, the "Grand Canyon" of the Black Forest, remains a unique experience. The Wutach, wild, unspoilt, the last natural and untamed river of the central German highlands. An island of untouched nature, in which the water has gouged out a deep ravine in the shell limestone. In the spring in particular, when the snow melts, the Wutach lives up to its name. Sometimes it changes its course without hesitation. Mountains of wood and scree are piled up on its banks. Rock walls are undercut, creating new gravel banks. In summer, the Wutach becomes more subdued. 15 miles of trekking then lie between the Lenzkirch Chapel and the Wutach mill. In order to preserve the ecological balance of the Wutach, the number of visitors is restricted. One overwhelming natural experience is the gorge: around 500 species of butterflies and over 1,200 species of plants, including many orchids. Over 100 species of birds also live here, including kestrels and kingfishers.
But the Black Forest is not simply nature at its virgin best, there are also many towns. Bad Wildbad, for example. People have been coming here seeking a cure for over 600 years. Its water helps against exhaustion, and health which has fallen out of balance, it is said. Even rheumatic saddle horses of the nobility are said to have been cured here.
Or Freudenstadt, the highest town in the Black Forest, with the largest market square in Germany. Duke Friedrich I of Württemberg had it laid out in 1599 – and the town around it. He actually planned to build his Palace in the centre of the square, but it was never built. Protestant religious refugees were to follow the ducal promise of a better life, and help the region to prosper.
The sophisticated beauty is Baden-Baden, for a long time the summer retreat of the moneyed classes and the aristocracy. Princes came here to pick out a potential bride. Counts lost their fortune and their honour in the casino. Generals recuperated under the Roman-Irish dome of the "Friedrichsbad". Mark Twain saw through the blithe goings-on of the spa guests, "full of pretence and pomposity".
The Swabian-Alemannic "Fasnet" or "Fasnacht" (~ carnival) however gets by completely without pomposity. In the Black Forest, "Fasnet" is a rustic festival. More colourful than splendid. Down-to-earth and ribald, full of ancient rituals. From "schmotzigen Dunschtig" (~ dirty Thursday) to Ash Wednesday, men and women are transformed into shaggy-headed mythical creatures, lively jesters and witches with horrible masks, which here are called "Larven". The air reverberates to the noise of rattles, the clatter of the nutshells against the costumes and the sound of the bells. In Schramberg, some of the more daring men attempt to toboggan down the Schiltach in rickety washtubs. In Rottweil, the fools jump through the "Black Gate". In Elzach, the flame-red "Schuttig" parade through the streets. Every town and village has its own stories, rituals and costumes, which are handed down from generation to generation.
Despite the old traditions, turmoil and tourism, one comes again and again to a lonely forest clearing, to silent lakes, picturesque corners and healthy air. One third of all spas and health resorts with a therapeutic climate are located in the stimulating climate of the Black Forest, where the attraction of the climate is provided by the pronounced temperature differences at these altitudes, the long hours of sunshine and the pure air.
Whether trekking through the sombre pines, through narrow gorges, over moors or sun-drenched meadows, whether letting the far gaze sweep over mountain and valley to the "Schwarzwald Hochstraße" or the "Westweg", whether negotiating snow-covered cross-country skiing trails, basking in warm thermal springs or enjoying the Black Forest gateau, that powerful combination of cream, cherries and biscuit soaked in schnaps. Whether on the shores of the Mummelsee or Titisee, in the Kinzigtal or on the Hornisgrinde, the Black Forest is still as untouched and primeval, wild and romantic as ever. Its charm and magic are inescapable.

La Forêt Noire

Iris Lemanczyk

Une forêt de sapins sombres. Dans le contre-jour, les montagnes et les arbres forment un décor ténébreux, d'une noirceur presque totale. La Forêt Noire. Ce pays rude, plus haut plateau d'Allemagne après les Alpes, s'étend sur plus de 160 km entre les villes de Pforzheim et de Bâle. Rude mais aussi riant et idyllique, bucolique et primitif. Avec des gorges aux parois verticales à travers lesquelles dévalent des torrents furieux et des lacs aux eaux d'un bleu profond lovés au cœur de doux vallons ; avec des formations rocheuses bizarroïdes, des cascades spectaculaires, des sommets montagneux pelés, des marais asséchés ; avec l'odeur pénétrante du sapin et de la résine ; avec la brume qui s'élève lentement vers le soleil, renvoyant ainsi momentanément les esprits de la forêt à leur tanière. La lumière joue avec le paysage, créant des décors de plus en plus enchanteurs : des collines d'un vert tendre, des prairies de montagne luxuriantes, des vallées romantiques ...

Pourtant les noms des vallées, des rivières et autres lieux disséminés entre les forêts de sapins et d'épicéas sont tout sauf charmants et idylliques : «Höllental» (vallée de l'enfer), «Nothschrei» (cri de détresse), «Zuflucht» (refuge), «Siehdichfür» (prends garde), «Bärental» (vallée des ours), «Wutach» (torrent en furie) ou «Wolfach» (torrent du loup) sont bien loin des adjectifs couramment utilisés pour décrire le charme d'une région. Pendant longtemps, la Forêt Noire est restée une contrée sauvage, une forêt vierge, une mer de bois impénétrable.

Pour les Romains, la Forêt Noire était un obstacle déplaisant, inaccessible, voire même sinistre, un monde peuplée d'élans, d'ours et d'aurochs. La seule chose qu'ils apprécient ici, ce sont en fait les sources thermales qui jaillissent à la périphérie occidentale de la Forêt Noire. Ils ne se contentent pas d'ailleurs de camper à proximité de ces sources, ils fondent également des hameaux et des villes tout autour comme Ettlingen, Baden-Baden et Badenweiler pour n'en citer que quelques-unes.

Des moines courageux ont été parmi les premiers colons à oser s'aventurer dans cette contrée sauvage, lugubre et inquiétante. Le couvent de Saint-Trudpert dans la vallée de Münster, l'une des plus anciennes traces de colonisation dans cette région, apparaît pour la première fois dans les chroniques au 7ème siècle. D'autres monastères sont fondés dans les années et les siècles qui suivent à Hirsau, Alpirsbach et Enzklösterle. Après l'église, c'est la noblesse qui tente ensuite de s'approprier certaines parties de la Forêt Noire. Les Zähringers notamment s'établissent dans la «Nigra Silva» parsemée de sapins. La population commence alors à déboiser les lisières des forêts, prenant le bois dont elle a besoin soit pour construire, soit pour se chauffer. Ce sont à cette époque les deux rôles essentiels de la forêt, considérée au reste comme superflue. C'est au 14ème siècle que débute une exploitation ciblée du capital forestier et que sont ainsi construites les premières scieries ainsi que les premières verreries.

Le commerce du bois connaît plus tard un essor colossal. Le seul moyen d'acheminer ces gigantesques troncs d'arbre depuis les forêts de montagne jusqu'aux marchés sur les berges du Neckar et du Rhin était d'utiliser les rivières et les fleuves. Les troncs abattus étaient d'abord traînés par des chevaux jusqu'à la rive de la rivière flottable la plus proche : les petits troncs étaient simplement jetés à l'eau et descendaient la rivière avant d'être récupérés en un point précis, mais les immenses troncs étaient généralement assemblés par les flotteurs de bois qui sautaient ensuite sur ces radeaux et descendaient les divers biefs, contournaient des méandres de la rivière en passant parfois sur le lit rocheux de la rivière. Un métier dangereux qui exigeaient des hommes une force énorme et une grande habilité. Ce n'est pas pour rien d'ailleurs que les flotteurs de bois étaient généreusement payés par les propriétaires forestiers. Les troncs débités étaient en général destinés à la Hollande, grande consommatrice de bois pour la construction navale. C'est d'ailleurs la raison pour laquelle on appelait les gigantesques troncs de 20 m maximum des «Hollandais».

Le métier de porteur d'horloges, qui forçait celui qui l'exerçait à beaucoup voyager, est un autre métier typique de la Forêt Noire. Les horloges fabriquées en Forêt Noire s'exportaient déjà très bien au 18ème siècle et il n'était pas rare de rencontrer l'un de ces porteurs avec une horloge sur son dos à Paris, Istanbul ou Saint-Pétersbourg. Franz Ketterer de Schönwald a inventé vers 1740 le premier coucou au cours d'un hiver terriblement long où il était désœuvré. L'histoire selon laquelle un maître-horloger aurait ramené chez lui un oisillon tombé du nid, un coucou, pour le soigner a toutefois la vie dure, aujourd'hui encore. Elle raconte qu'à force d'entendre l'oiseau crier toujours «coucou» à chaque heure pleine, l'horloger aurait fini par lui sculpter sa propre horloge. D'autres affirment en revanche que le coucou étant considéré comme un porte-bonheur, il a tout naturellement fini par trouver une place dans les horloges. Quoi qu'il en soit, cette invention a permis de créer de nombreux emplois dans une région dont les seules ressources étaient son bois et son bon air.

Plus tard, l'avènement du chemin de fer permet un transport plus rapide des horloges : elles sont expédiées en train jusqu'aux ports d'où elles sont exportées en bateau vers les quatre coins du monde. En 1893, la «cuckoo clock» est la vedette de l'exposition industrielle de Chicago : les Américains découvrent alors la «Black Forest».

Ernest Hemingway part pêcher la truite à Triberg pendant sa jeunesse. Mark Twain se promène à travers la Forêt Noire où il s'intéresse à sa nature et à ses habitants. Absolument fasciné par ce qu'il découvre, il écrit : «Si on a le malheur de commencer à dévaler ici une pente, il est alors impossible de s'arrêter avant d'atteindre le fond. Imaginez-vous que les paysans sont ici obligés de travailler dans des champs si pentus qu'on peut dire au mieux que ceux-ci sont un peu plus raides qu'une échelle mais qu'ils le sont moins qu'un toit mansardé. Et pourtant, ils y arrivent.»

Les versants très pentus dans cette région possédaient et possèdent encore un atout de taille : ils se prêtent en effet parfaitement à la pratique du ski et de la luge, du moins en descente. En 1891, l'explorateur norvégien du Pôle Nord Fridtjof Nansen fait découvrir le ski aux habitants de la Forêt Noire. Les facteurs sont les premiers à bénéficier de ce nouvel équipement afin de pouvoir atteindre les fermes très isolées même en hiver. La même année, des amateurs enthousiastes de ce nouveau sport créent le tout premier club de ski, le «Ski-Club Todtnau».

A la même époque environ, le fermier, aubergiste et bricoleur Robert Winterhalder de Schollach perfectionne une technique de traction utilisée dans les moulins et dépose le brevet d'invention d'un «système permettant aux skieurs et aux lugeurs de remonter les pentes enneigées au moyen d'un câble en boucle» – le premier remonte-pente de l'histoire est né. Il ne se trouve pas à Davos en Suisse ou à Garmisch en Allemagne mais sur les terres de la ferme de Winterhalder, la «Schneckenhof», et il peut remonter les lugeurs et les skieurs sur 280 m.

Le tourisme hivernal dans la Forêt Noire acquiert alors une nouvelle dimension. Actuellement, le Feldberg, point culminant de la Forêt Noire à 1493 m d'altitude, attire en hiver des milliers de skieurs de piste, de skieurs de fond et de snowboarders. Le tourisme est devenu ici un phénomène de masse, bien loin du charme irrésistible des chaînes de montagnes couvertes de neige, de la solitude et du calme.

En été aussi, lorsque la Forêt Noire se transforme en un paradis pour les randonneurs, il faut bien souvent s'enfoncer loin dans la forêt pour trouver calme et solitude. Le tourisme, né à l'origine d'un engouement romantique pour la nature, a gagné peu à peu toute la région, même les contrées autrefois impraticables et isolées.

Malgré tout, une randonnée à travers les Gorges de Wutach, le «Grand Canyon» de la Forêt Noire, reste pour tous une expérience unique et extraordinaire. La Wutach, cours d'eau sauvage et bucolique, est le dernier torrent indompté des chaînes allemandes de moyenne montagne. Une oasis naturelle encore intacte dans laquelle l'eau a creusé un profond ravin à travers le calcaire conchylien. Au printemps notamment, à l'époque de la fonte des neiges, la Wutach fait honneur à son nom car il lui arrive parfois de se mettre en colère et de quitter brusquement son lit, amoncelant des tas de bois et d'éboulis sur ses rives et rongeant des pans de parois rocheuses, créant ainsi de nouveaux bancs de graviers. En été, la Wutach s'assagit et suit calmement son cours. 24 km séparent ensuite Lenzkirch-Kappel du moulin de Wutach. Afin ne pas mettre en péril l'équilibre écologique de cette rivière, le nombre de visiteurs est limité. Les gorges offrent un spectacle naturel époustouflant au milieu duquel on dénombre jusqu'à 500 espèces de papillons environ, 1200 plantes différentes dont de nombreuses orchidées et plus d'une centaine d'oiseaux divers comme par exemple la crécerelle et le martin-pêcheur.

La Forêt Noire n'est pas seulement une idylle naturelle, elle fait également la part belle aux villes comme Bad Wildbad par exemple qui, il y a 600 ans, attirait déjà les malades qui espéraient être guéris ici de leurs maux. On dit que ses eaux ont un effet bénéfique sur les personnes souffrant d'épuisement ou d'un déséquilibre de la santé. On raconte même que les nobles faisaient soigner ici leurs montures percluses de rhumatismes.

Ou encore Freudenstadt, sur le plus haut plateau de la Forêt Noire, qui peut s'enorgueillir de posséder la plus grande place de marché de toute l'Allemagne dont la construction – tout comme celle de la ville tout autour – est ordonnée en 1599 par le duc Frédéric Ier de Wurtemberg. Il envisageait en fait d'ériger son palais au milieu de la place, mais ce projet n'a jamais pu être mené à bien. Les exilés protestants victimes de la persécution religieuse devaient suivre la promesse du duc d'une vie meilleure et contribuer ainsi à l'essor de la région.

Baden-Baden, ville mondaine par excellence, a longtemps été la résidence d'été de la noblesse d'argent et de l'aristocratie : elle est le rendez-vous des princes à la recherche d'une épouse, des comtes qui perdent leur fortune et leur honneur au casino et des généraux qui reprennent des forces dans les thermes romains-irlandais du «Friedrichsbad». Mark Twain a perçu à jour l'animation joyeuse des curistes où «tout n'est que prétention et manières pompeuses».

Le carnaval souabe-alémanique «Fasnet» ou «Fastnacht» ne saurait quant à lui se dérouler sans ce déploiement de pompe. Dans la Forêt Noire, le carnaval est une fête paysanne, plus haute en couleurs que resplendissante. Terre à terre et grivoise, pleine de rituels séculaires. Du «schmotzigen Dunschtig » ou Jeudi Gras jusqu'au Mercredi des Cendres, hommes et femmes se travestissent en d'hirsutes créatures fabuleuses, en bouffons pleins d'entrain et en sorcières portant d'horribles masques, appelés ici «Larve». L'air est empli du bruit des crécelles, du cliquetis des coquilles de noix contre les costumes et du tintamarre des clochettes. A Schramberg, quelques hommes audacieux tentent de descendre la Schiltach dans des baquets chancelants. A Rottweil, les «Narren» ou bouffons sautent à travers la «Porte Noire». A Elzach, les «Schuttig» d'un rouge flamboyant paradent à travers les ruelles. Chaque ville, chaque village a ses histoires, ses rites et ses «déguisements» hérités de génération en génération.

Malgré les vieilles traditions, l'animation et le tourisme, on trouve toujours une clairière solitaire, un lac paisible, un coin pittoresque et du bon air. Un tiers des stations thermales se situe dans le climat vivifiant de la Forêt Noire qui tire ses qualités des fortes différences de température à ces altitudes, du long ensoleillement et de l'air pur.

Que l'on marche à travers des forêts de sapins sombres, à travers d'étroites gorges, des marais ou des prairies inondées de soleil, que l'on laisse son regard voler au loin au-delà des montagnes et des vallées sur la «Schwarzwald Hochstraße» ou le «Westweg», que l'on emprunte des pistes de ski de fond couvertes de neige, que l'on se prélasse dans la chaleur des sources thermales ou que l'on déguste une Forêt-Noire, cette pâtisserie composée de crème fouettée, de cerises à l'eau-de-vie et de copeaux de chocolat, que ce soit sur les rives des lacs Mummelsee ou Titisee, dans la Vallée de Kinzig ou sur le Hornisgrinde, la Forêt Noire reste un pays bucolique et intact, sauvage et romantique : impossible de se soustraire à son charme et à sa magie.

Bad Säckingen Grenzbrücke über den Rhein

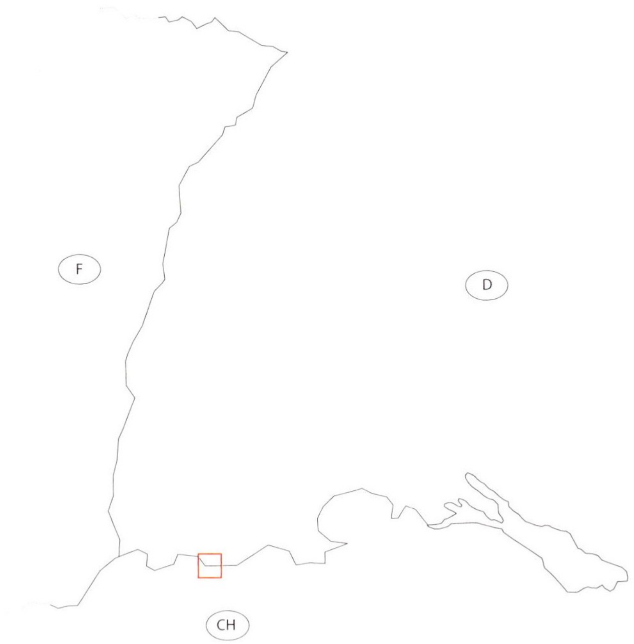

1

BUNDESREPUBLIK
DEUTSCHLAND

Waldshut Fußgängerzone

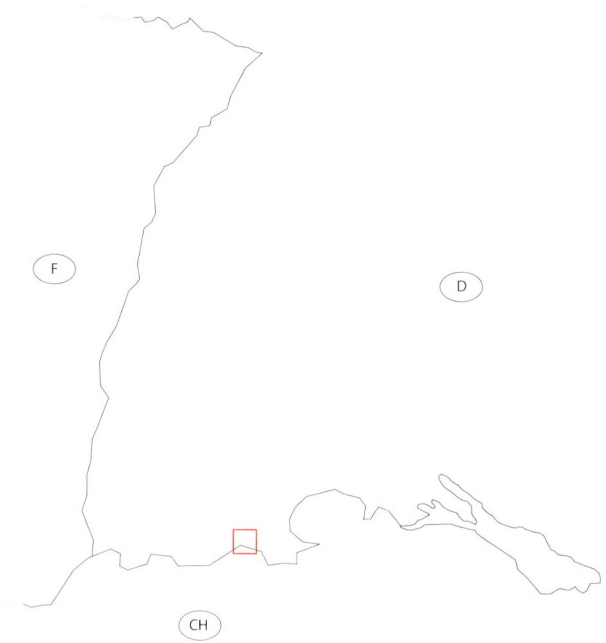

WALDSHUTER
UHREN • OPTIK
HERZOG

Wittenschwand bei Dachsberg Klosterweiher

3

St. Blasien Domkirche

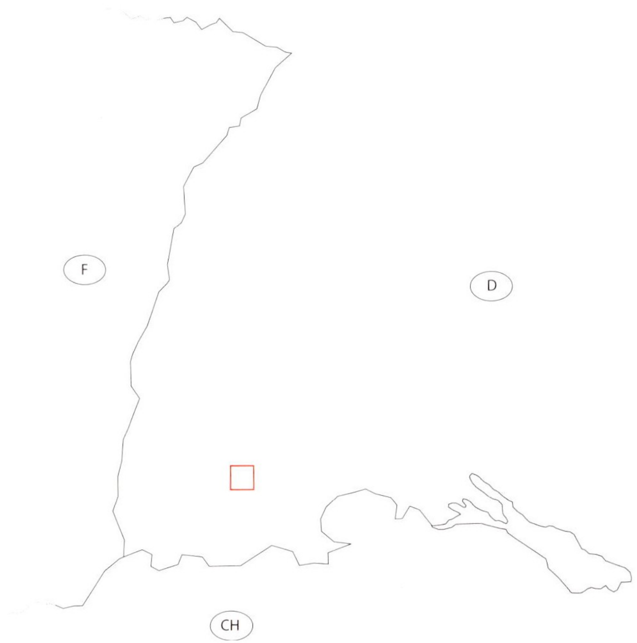

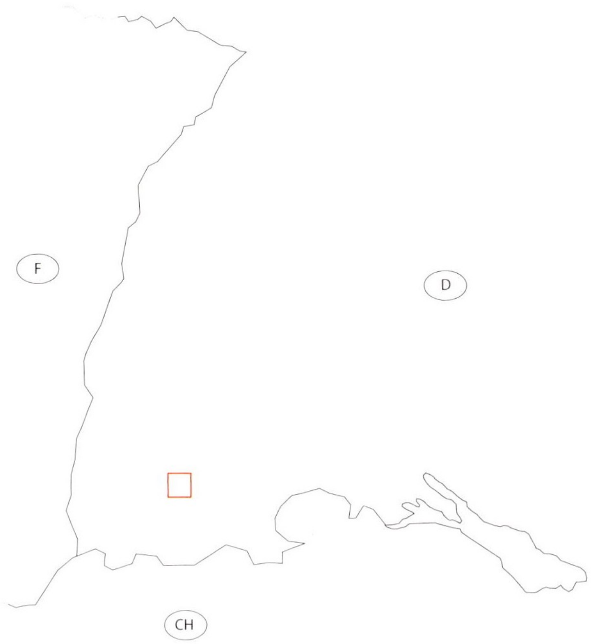
F
D
CH

Todtmoos
Glasträgerraum
Heimatmuseum

Auggen

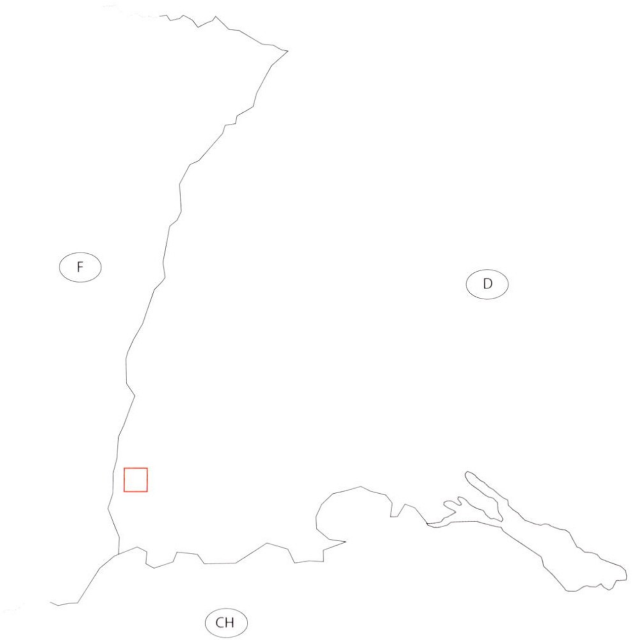

Münstertal Kloster St. Trudpert

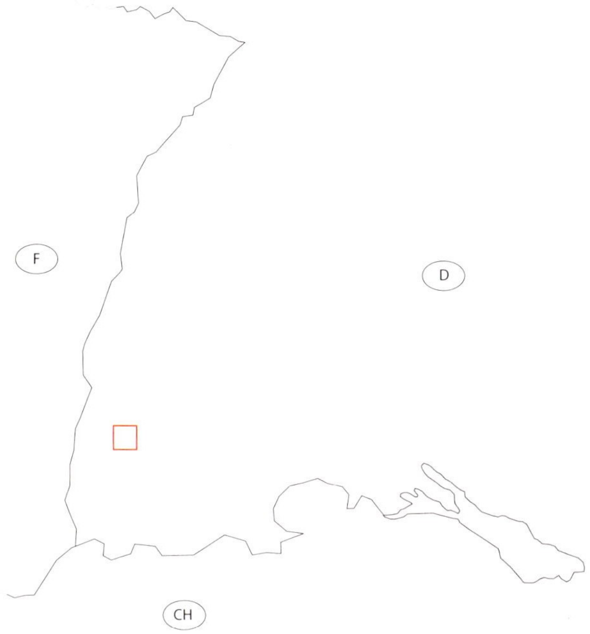

Münstertal-Stohren Strecke zum Schauinsland

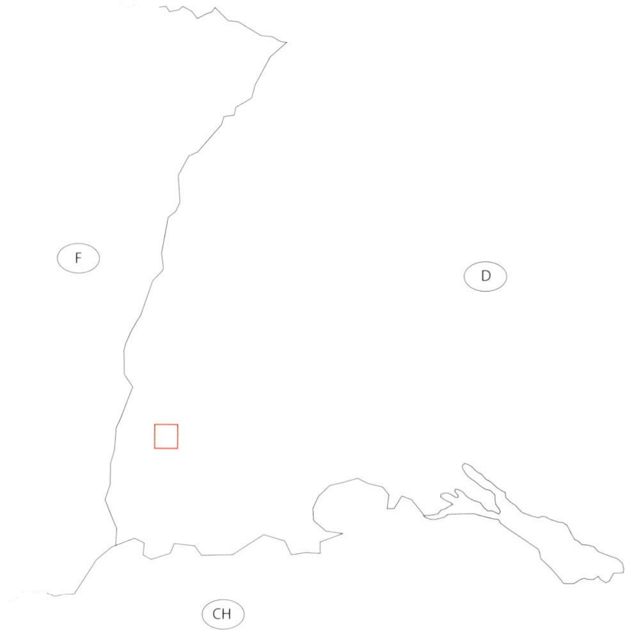

Wiedener Eck

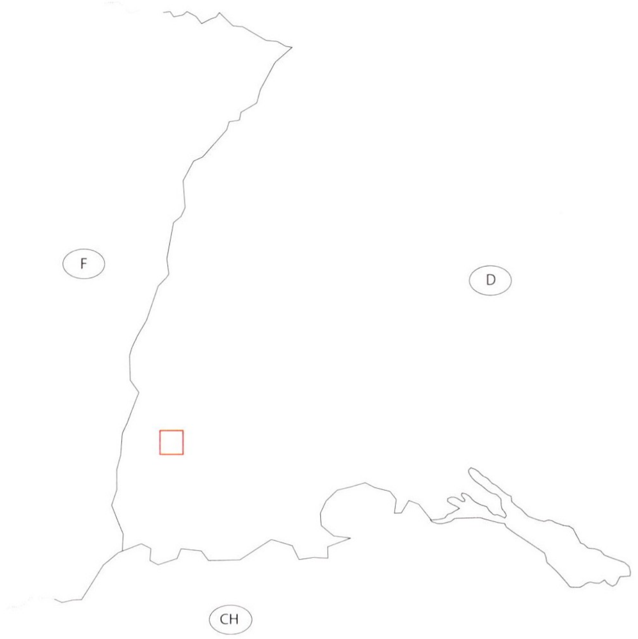

Schauinsland

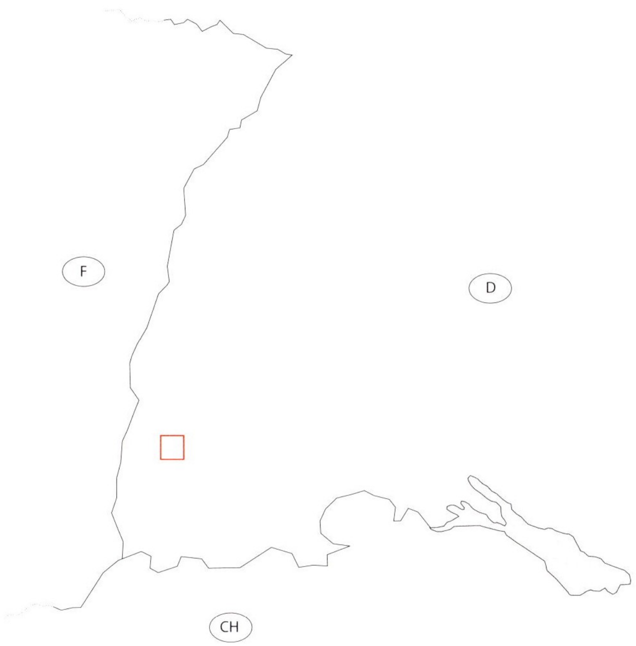

Feldberg

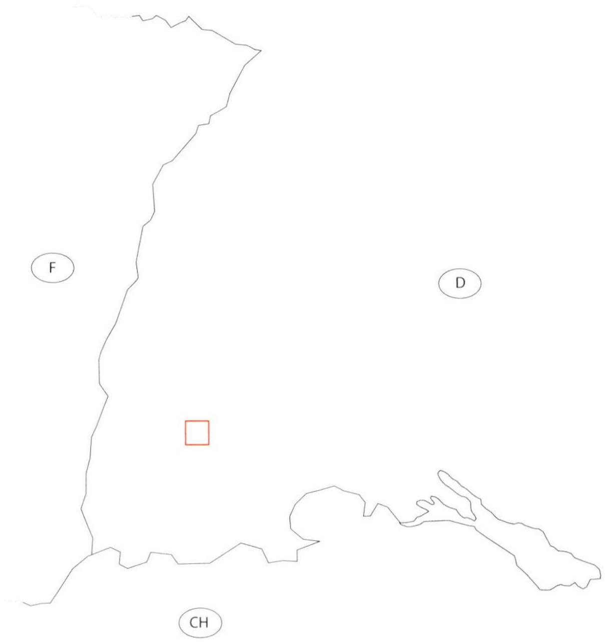

Schluchsee Gehöft Unterkrummen

Schluchsee Steinkunst am Ufer

Epfenhofen Museumsbahn

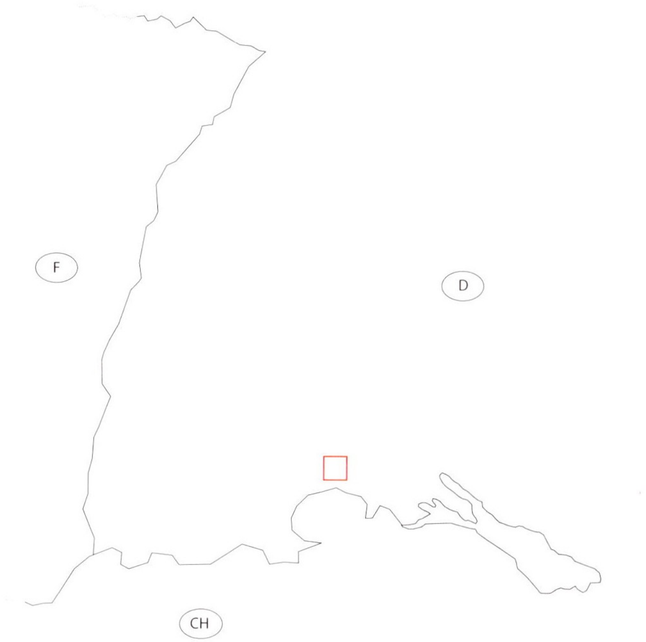

Wutachschlucht

Titisee Blick zum Feldberg

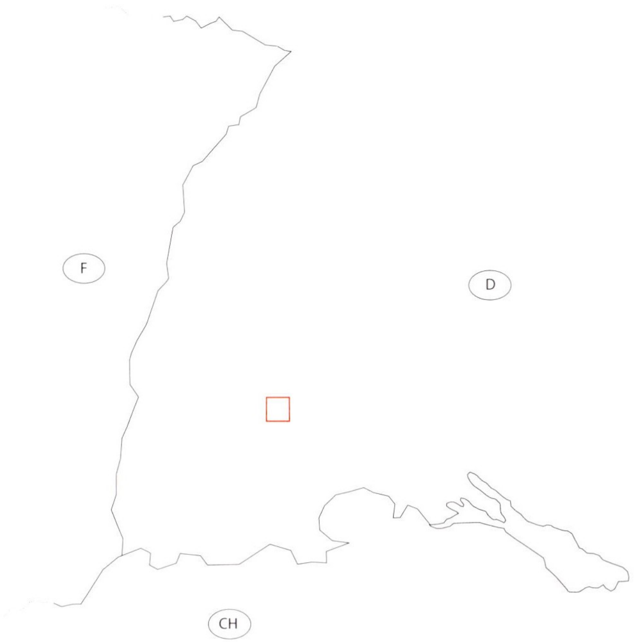

Titisee Blick vom Hochfirst

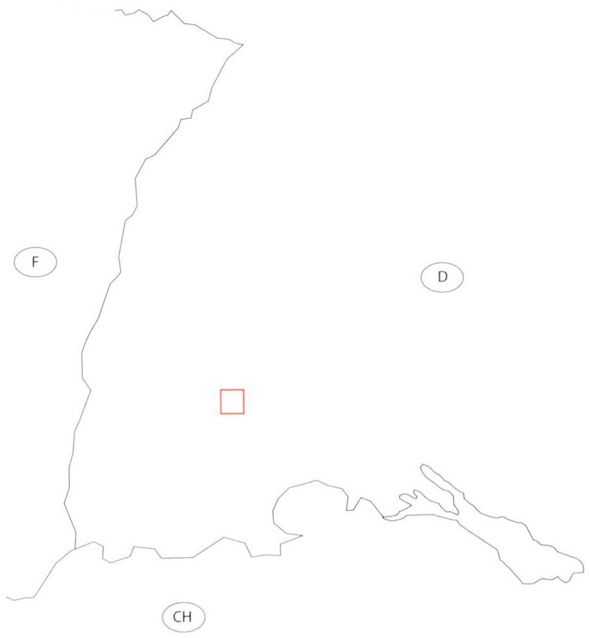

Titisee Ufer mit Schiffslände

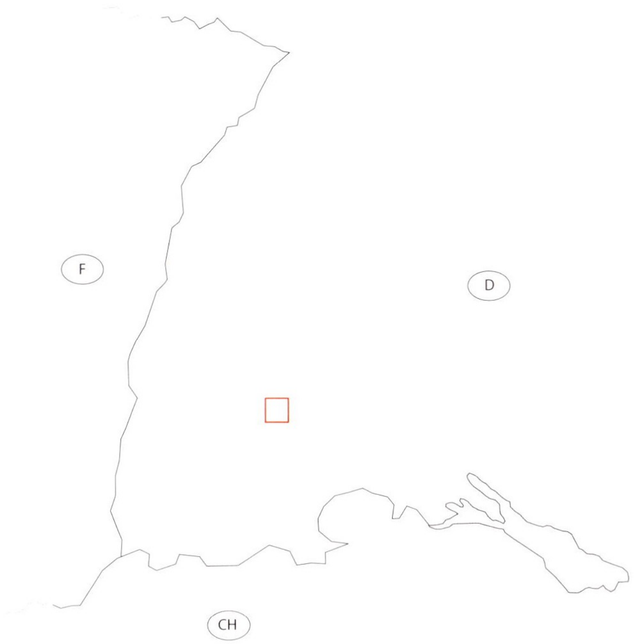

Freiburg Café am Münsterplatz

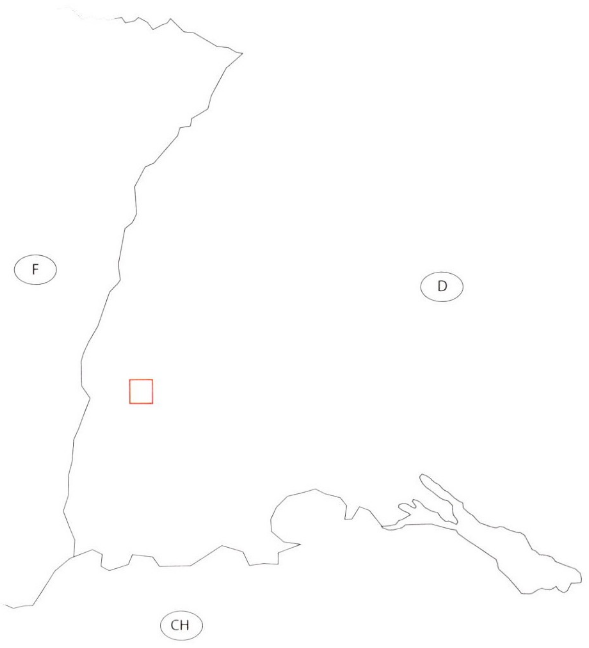

O'DWYER'S
IRISH
BEER GARDEN
OPEN FROM
7PM

Breitnau

Breitnau

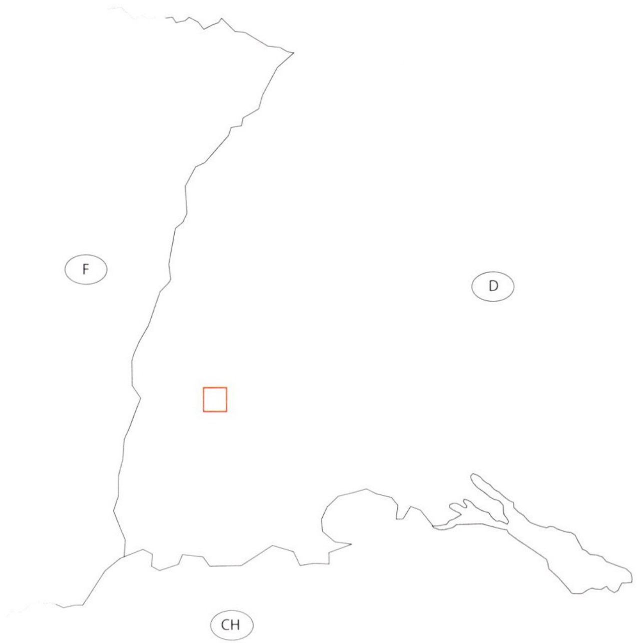

Breitnau

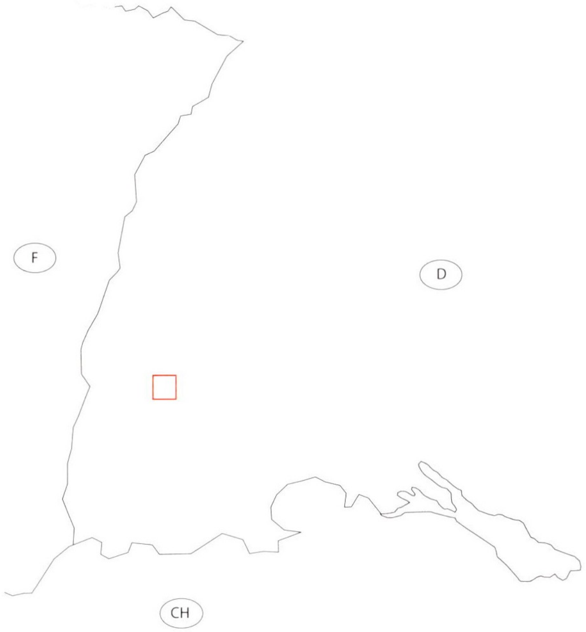

22

Thurner

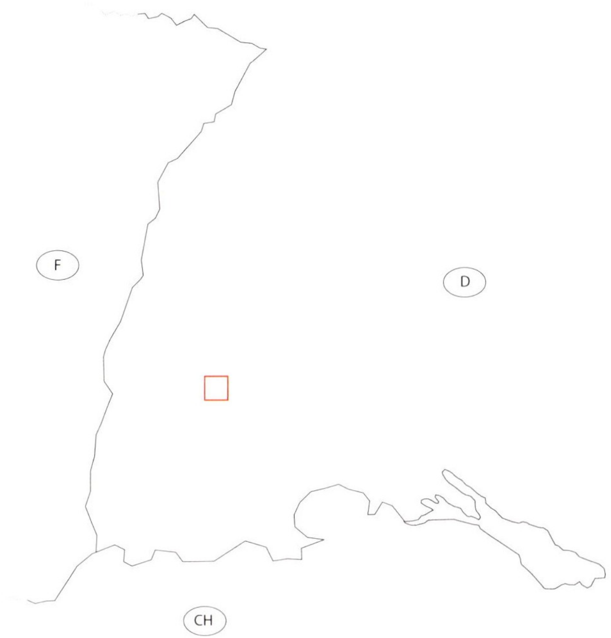

Waldau

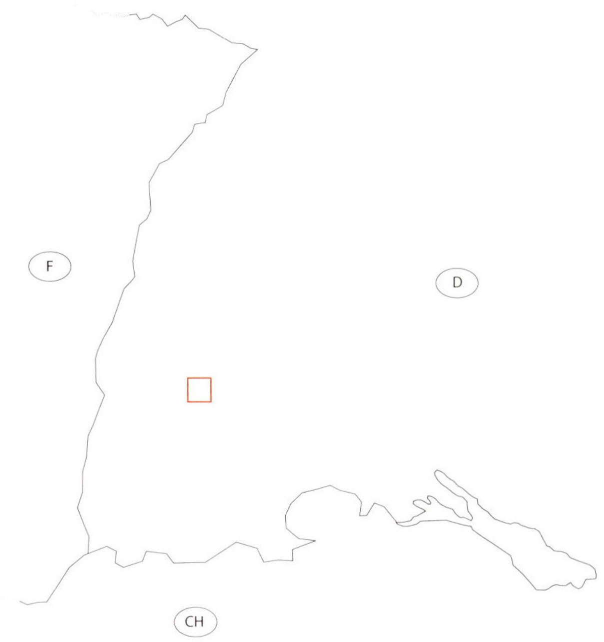

Waldau Blick vom Lachenhäusle

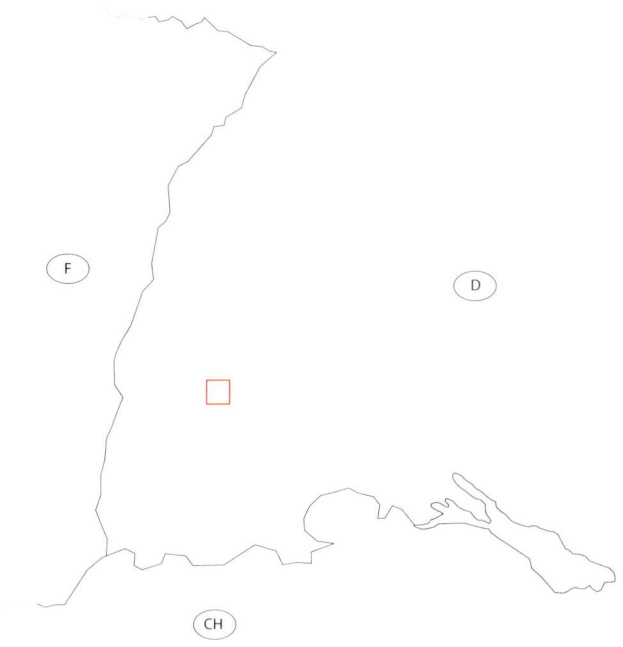

Wildgutachtal

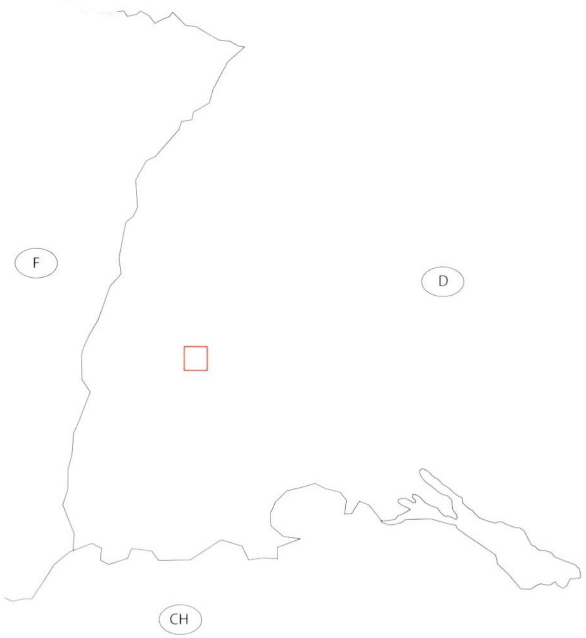

Furtwangen Hexenlochmühle bei Neukirch

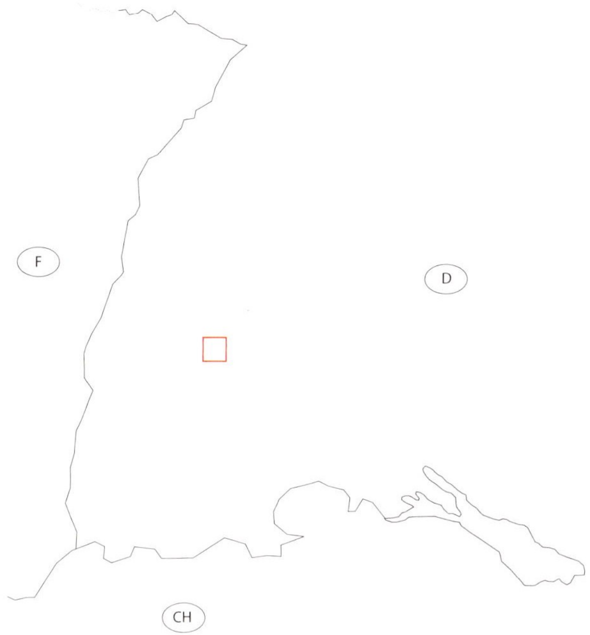

KUCKUCKSUHREN
EIGENE HERSTELLUNG
SCHWARZWÄLDER
SPEZIALITÄTEN

Furtwangen Martinskapelle bei Katzensteig

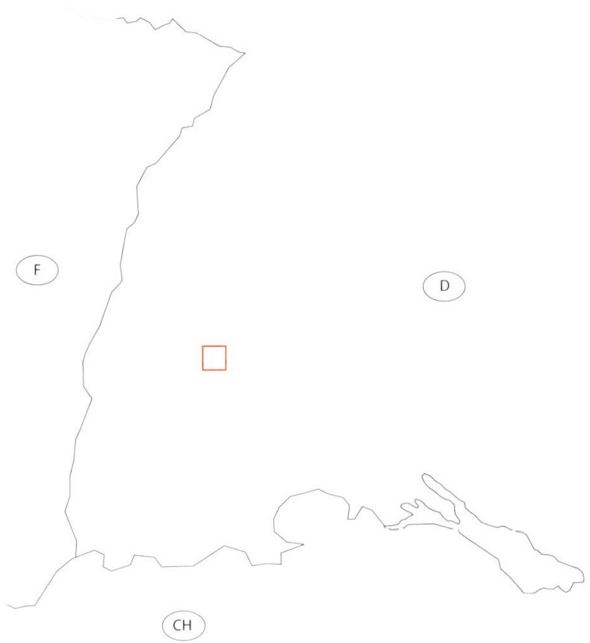

28

Wolterdingen

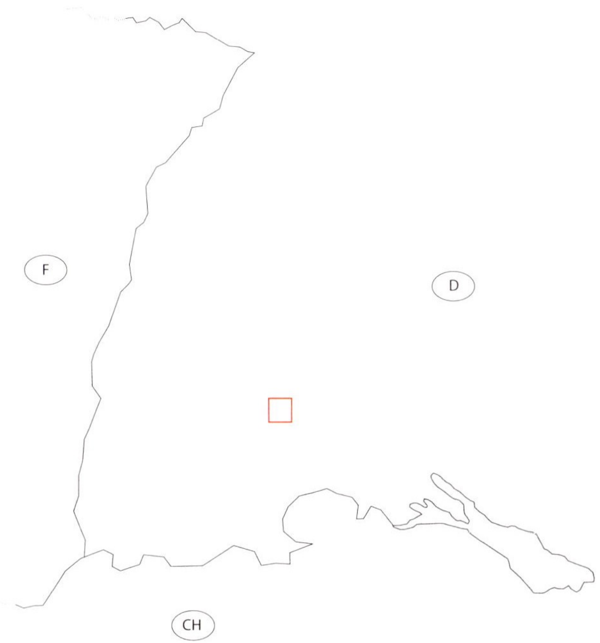

Vöhrenbach Nadelwald

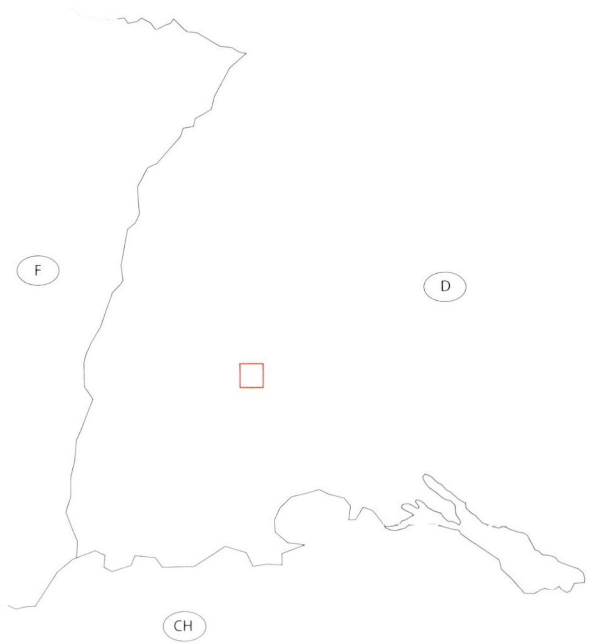

Triberg Triberger Wasserfall

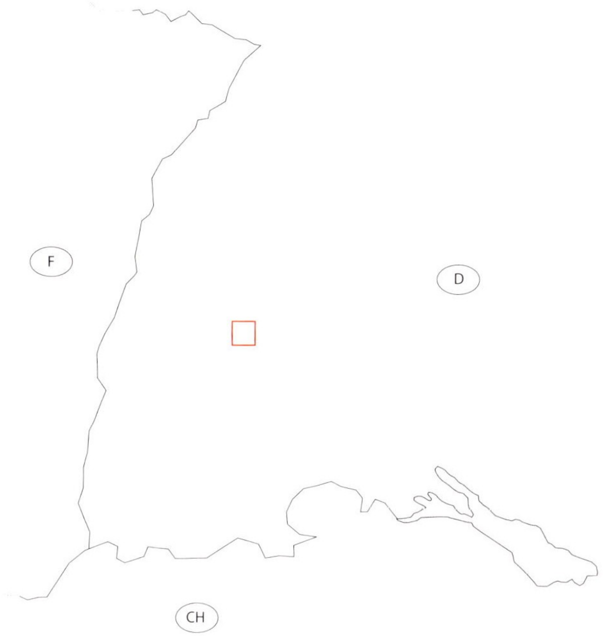

Obersimonswald Hausfassade

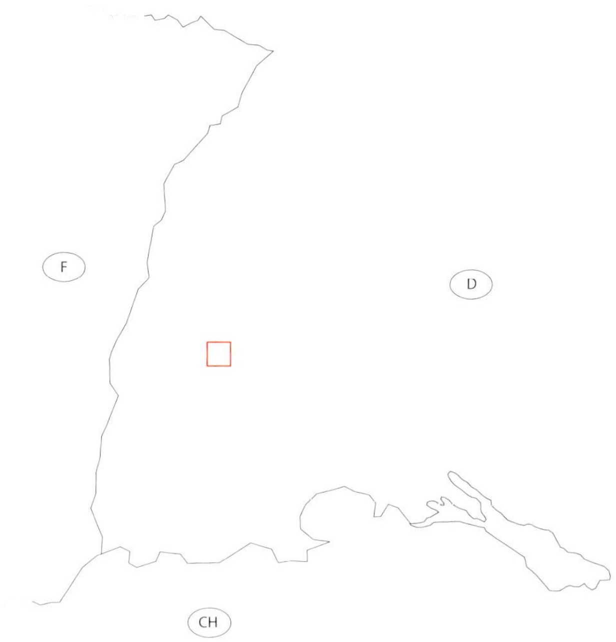

Kandelspitze bei Waldkirch Gipfelhäuschen

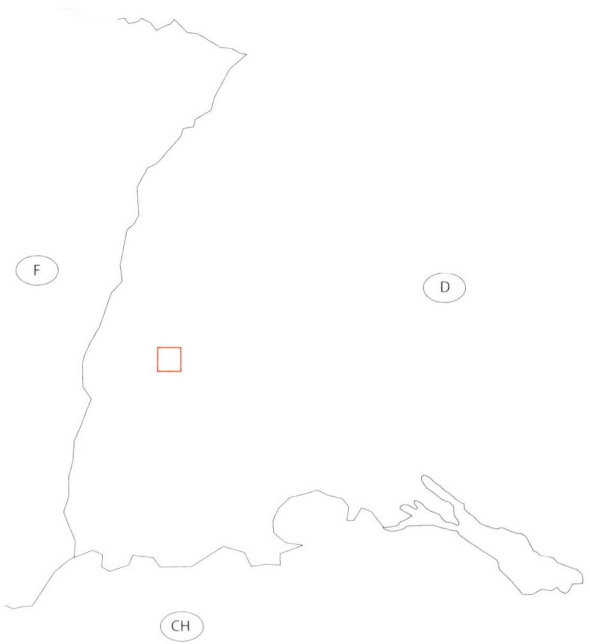

Sexau Ruine Hochburg

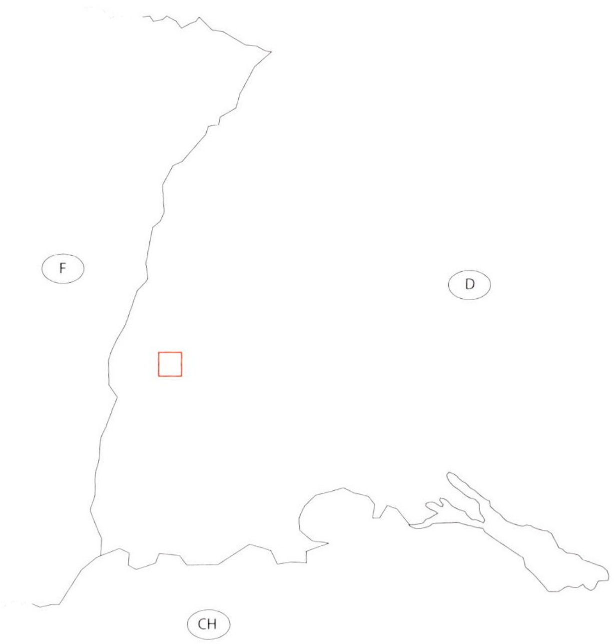

Welschensteinach bei Haslach

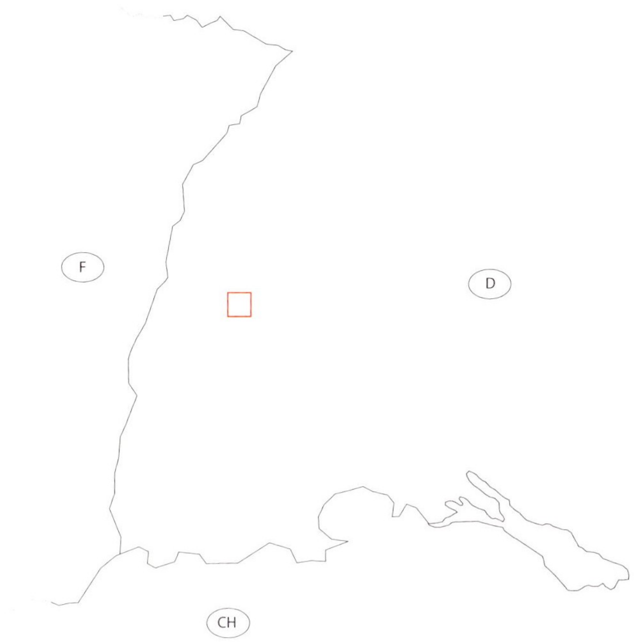

Mühlenbach vor Haslach Fronleichnamsprozession

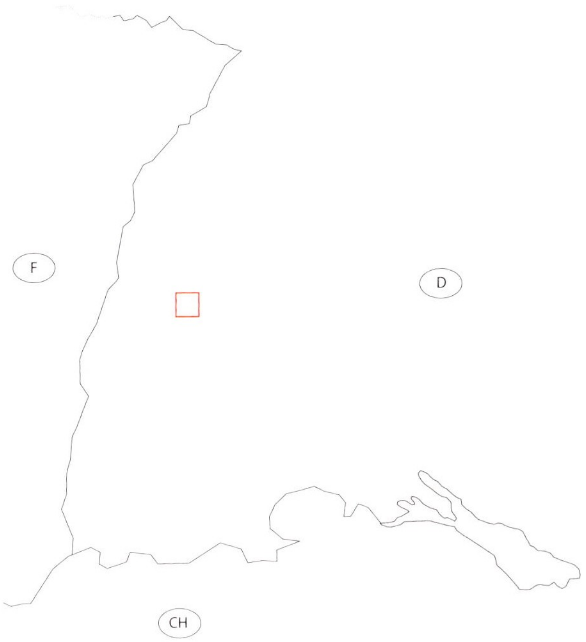

Gutach Vogtsbauernhöfe

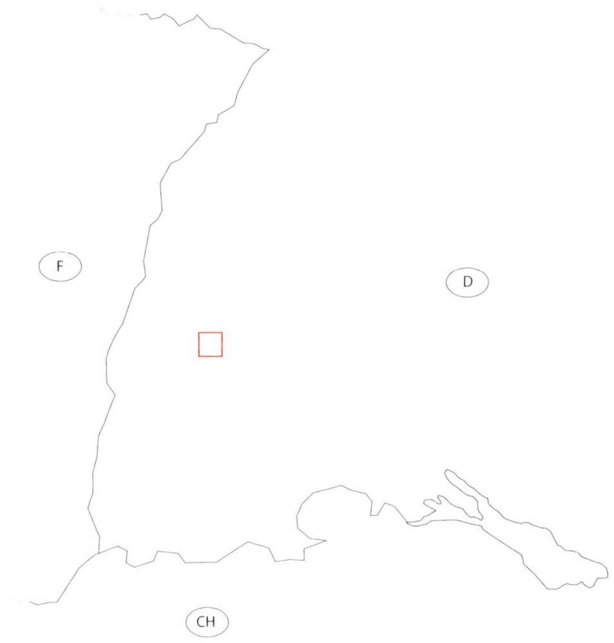

Schiltach Marktplatz

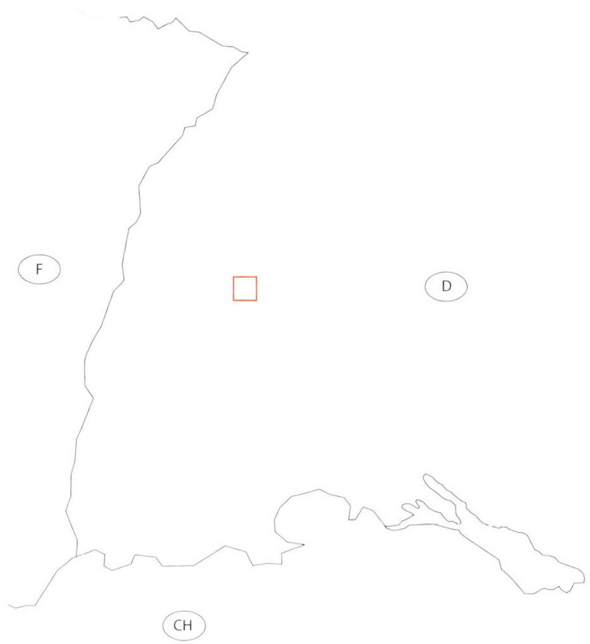

Schanno
Schanno

Oberharmersbach

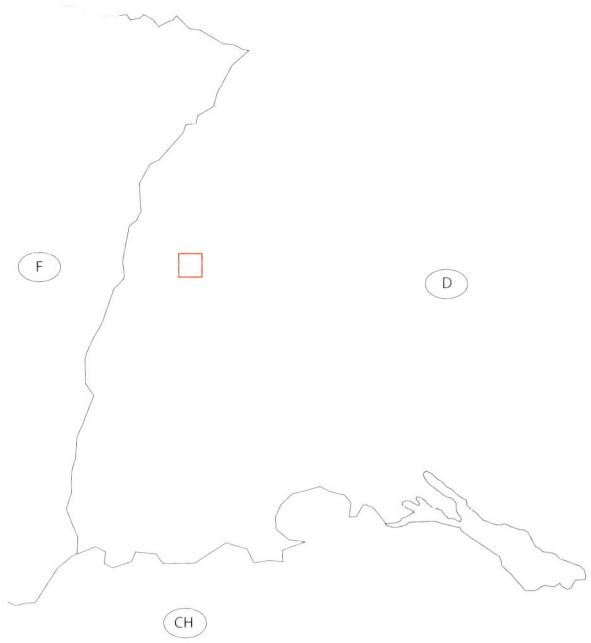

Glatt bei Sulz

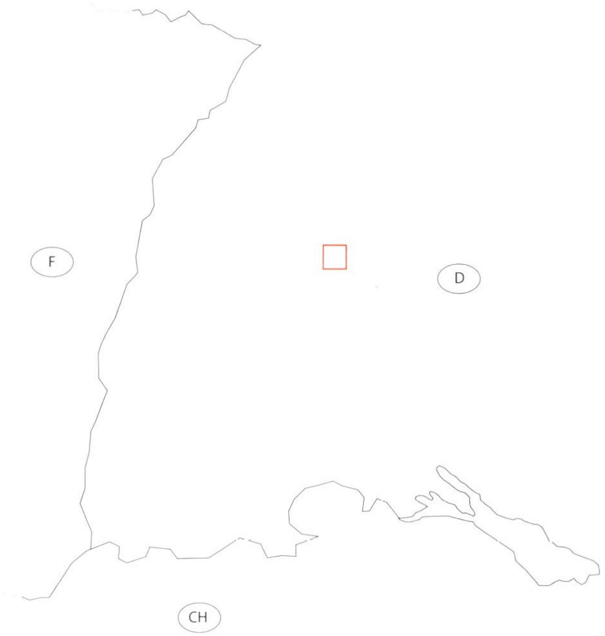

Altensteig Mittelalterlicher Dorfkern

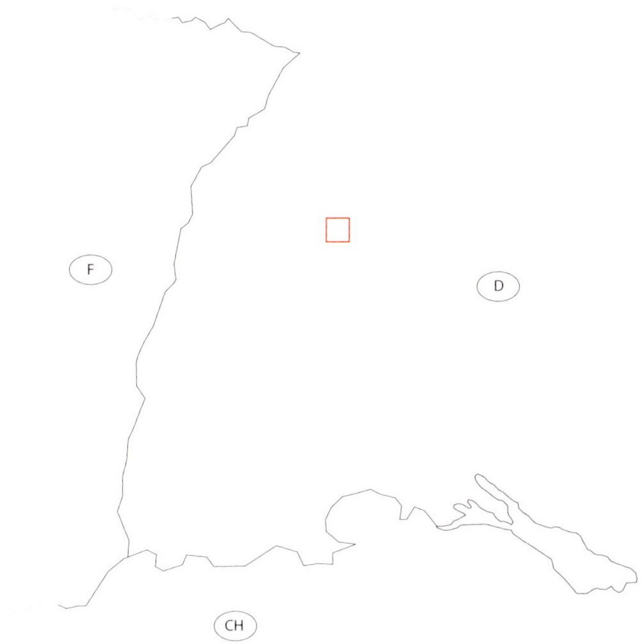

Schliffkopf

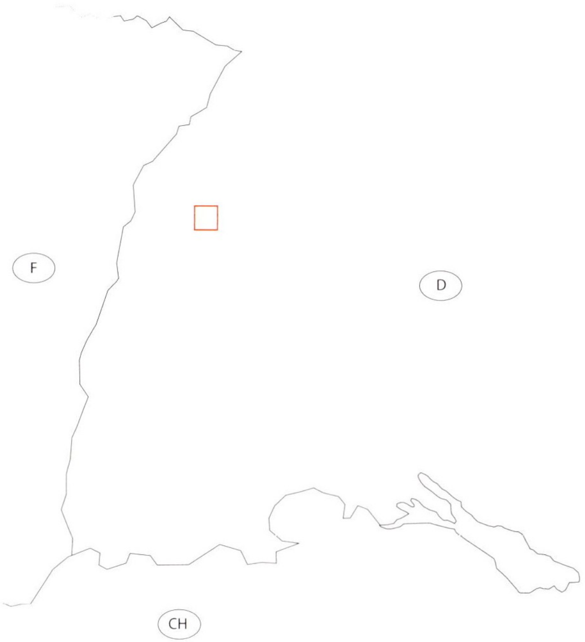

Schliffkopf

Ruhestein

Mummelsee

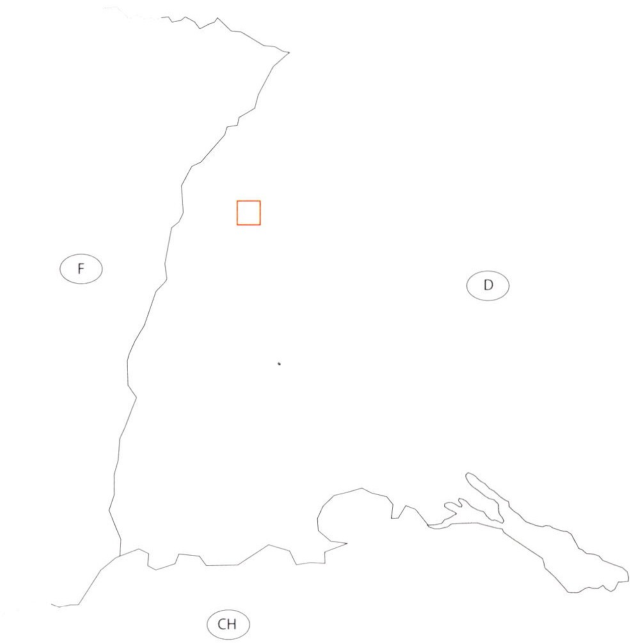

Seebach Kirschblüte

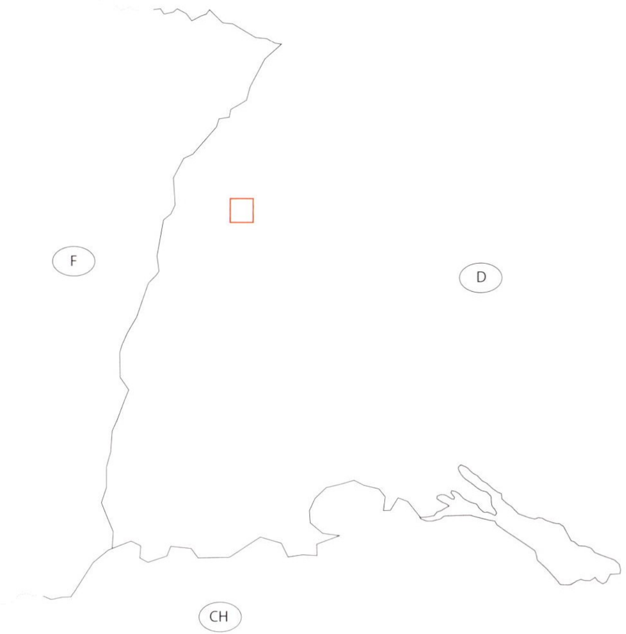

Ottenhöfen Blick ins Achertal

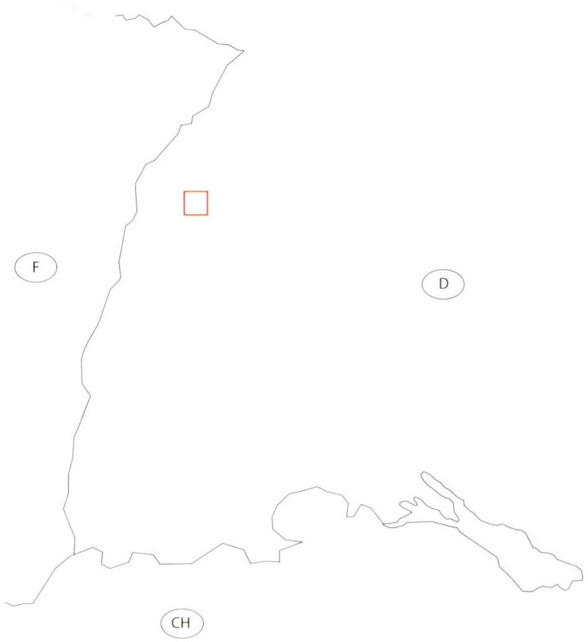

Baden-Baden Terrasse des Neuen Schlosses

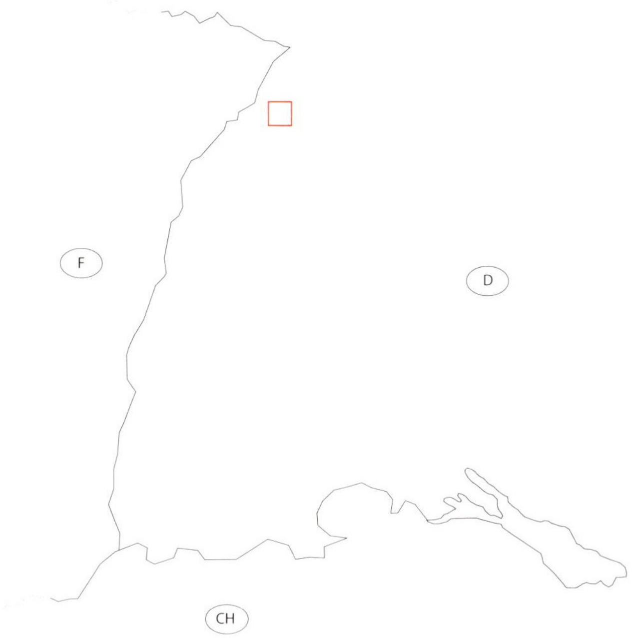

Schwarzenbach Talsperre bei Raumünzach

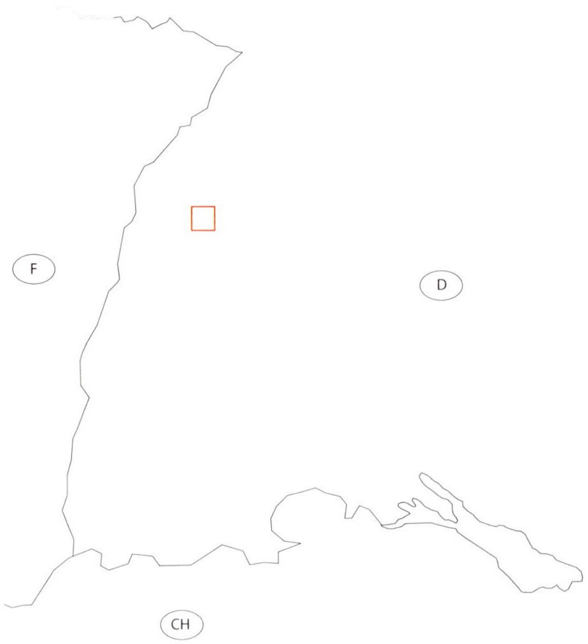

Reichental bei Weisenbach

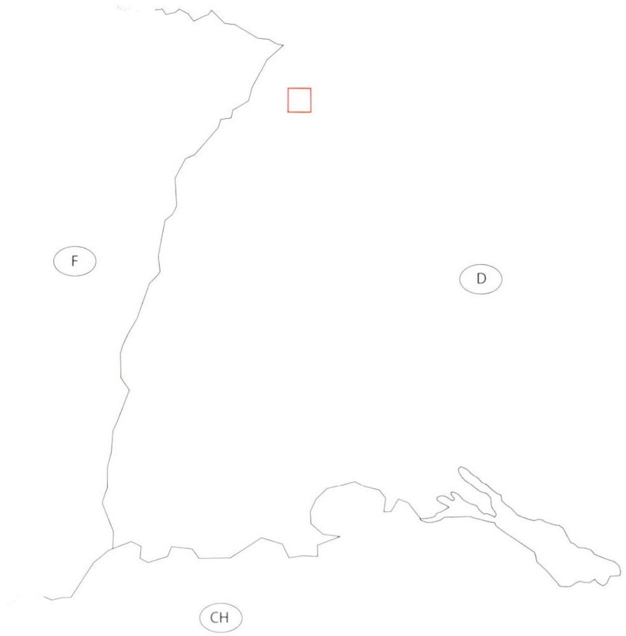

Zavelstein

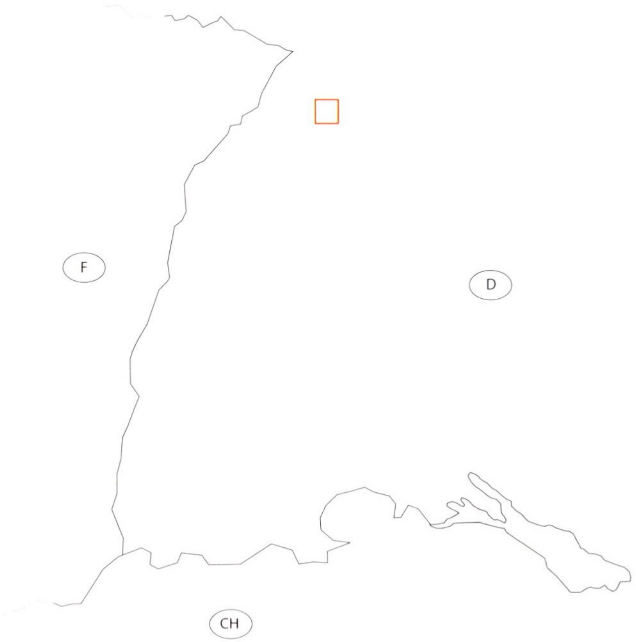

FUJI

HOLGER SPIERING wurde 1967 in Überlingen am Bodensee geboren. Er studierte Forstwissenschaft in Schweden, wo er auch zum ersten Mal mit der Panoramaphotographie in Berührung kam. Es folgten weitere Reisen im Rahmen seiner Diplom-Arbeit nach Mittelamerika und Neuseeland. 1997 kehrte er an den Bodensee zurück, wo er bis heute mit seiner Frau und seinen beiden Kindern lebt. Seitdem widmet sich Holger Spiering professionell der Panoramaphotographie; seine bevorzugten Themen sind der Bodensee und der Schwarzwald.

IRIS LEMANCZYK wurde 1964 in Kirchheim/Teck bei Stuttgart geboren. Nach dem Studium der Germanistik und Geographie lockte immer wieder die Ferne. Sie reiste um die Welt, schnupperte eine Zeit lang Zirkusluft, lebte in Namibia und besuchte für ein paar Monate Australien und Neuseeland. Dazwischen arbeitete sie als Zeitungs-Redakteurin bei der „Südwest Presse" in Ulm. Seit 1997 ist sie freiberuflich tätig, schreibt Kinder- und Jugendbücher sowie Sachbücher, verfasst Reiseberichte und ist als Dozentin für kreatives Schreiben tätig.

HOLGER SPIERING was born in Überlingen on the the Lake of Constance in 1967. He studied forestry in Sweden, where he also came in touch with panorama photography for the first time. Other travels in the course of his master's thesis led him to Central America and to New Zealand. In 1997, he returned to the Lake of Constance, where he still lives with his wife and two children. Holger Spiering has since made panorama photography his profession. His favourite subject is the Lake of Constance at all times of the day and in all seasons.

IRIS LEMANCZYK was born in 1964 in Kirchheim/Teck near Stuttgart. After studying German and geography, she gave way to the call of far-distant places. She travelled around the world, experienced the circus life for a time, lived in Namibia and spent several months in Australia and New Zealand. In between, she also learnt something more conventional: newspaper editing with the "Südwest Presse" in Ulm. Since 1997 she has worke as a freelancer, writing children's books and non-fiction and compiling travel reports, and also works as a lecturer on creative writing.

HOLGER SPIERING est né en 1967 à Überlingen au bord du lac de Constance. Il a fait des études de sylviculture en Suède où il a aussi découvert la photo panoramique. De nombreux voyages ont suivi dans le cadre de ses travaux universitaires, notamment en Amérique centrale eten Nouvelle-Zélande. En 1997 il revient au bord du lac de Constance où il vit actuellement avec sa femme et ses deux enfants. Depuis Holger Spiering se consacre sur le plan professionnel à la photo panoramique, son thème favori est le lac de Constance au gré des jours et des saisons.

IRIS LEMANCZYK est né en 1964 à Kirchheim/Teck près de Stuttgart. Après des études de philologie allemande et de géographie, elle voyage à travers le monde, séjourne pendant quelque temps dans un cirque, vit en Namibie et passe plusieurs mois en Australie et en Nouvelle-Zélande. Entre toutes ces occupations, elle travaille comme rédactrice journalistique au quotidien allemand « Südwest Presse » à Ulm. Depuis 1997, elle écrit des livres destinés à l'enfance et à la jeunesse ainsi que des livres d'essai. Elle rédige également des comptes rendus de voyage et dispense des cours de création littéraire.

In der EDITION PANORAMA BIBLIOTHEK erhältlich | Available in the EDITION PANORAMA BIBLIOTHEK | Également disponible dans la collection EDITION PANORAMA BIBLIOTHEK

Iceland	978-3-89823-189-5
New York	978-3-89823-392-7
Tibet	978-3-89823-197-8
Cuba	978-3-89823-355-2
La Habana, Cuba	978-3-89823-179-4
Australia	978-3-89823-284-5
Paris	978-3-89823-239-5
Budapest	978-3-89823-280-7
Jemen	978-3-89823-278-4
Patagonia	978-3-89823-360-6
Norway	978-3-89823-393-4
Wien	978-3-89823-380-4
Mallorca	978-3-89823-290-6
Dubai	978-3-89823-279-1
Toscana	978-3-89823-198-5
Schwarzwald	978-3-89823-395-8
Salzburg	978-3-89823-394-1
Amsterdam	978-3-89823-353-8
Berlin	978-3-89823-168-8
Hamburg	978-3-89823-283-8
India	978-3-89823-237-1
New Zealand	978-3-89823-359-0
Islas Canarias	978-3-89823-357-6
Bruxelles	978-3-89823-354-5
Frankfurt	978-3-89823-390-3
Österreich	978-3-89823-381-1
Lisboa	978-3-89823-358-3
California	978-3-89823-389-7
Heidelberg	978-3-89823-356-9
Bodensee	978-3-89823-282-1
Sylt	978-3-89823-363-7
Venezia	978-3-89823-238-8
Schweiz	978-3-89823-362-0
Sahara	978-3-89823-183-1
Roma	978-3-89823-361-3

A production by EDITION PANORAMA, Germany

Printed in Germany

EDITION PANORAMA GmbH
G7, 14 | D-68159 Mannheim
Telefon +49 (0)621 / 32 88 69 - 0
Fax +49 (0)621 / 32 88 69 - 20
www.editionpanorama.com
www.bodenseefotografie.de

ISBN: 978-3-89823-395-8

Concept: Bernhard & Sebastian Wipfler
Design: Edition Panorama | Diana May und Designgruppe Fanz & Neumayer | Marcus Bela Schmitt
Editorial department: Dr. Michael Barchet, Wolfgang Roth
Translations: Global-Text Fachübersetzungen, Heidelberg | Mark Woolfe, Jocelyne Abarca
Separations: EPS GmbH, Speyer
Printing: Passavia Druckservice GmbH & Co. KG, Passau
Bookbinding: Josef Spinner Großbuchbinderei GmbH, Ottersweier
Covermaterial: "Imperial" Book Cloth, BN International
Endpapers: "Freelife Merida Graphite" 140 g/m², Fedrigoni Group
Slipcase: Neudel Verpackungen GmbH, Neckarbischofsheim